Please visit us at ezramonson.com/gift to download our free coloring pages

IN AN ORDINARY HOUSE,
NOT FAR AWAY,
LIVED A FAMILY OF DINOSAURS:
MOM, DAD AND LITTLE DINO.

ONE DAY MOM AND DAD
DINOSAUR BOUGHT
A POTTY FOR DINO.

*Tip for parents: Explain to your toddler why you need a potty at home

THEY ASKED DINO TO SIT
ON THE POTTY.
SO HE DID.

*Tip for parents: We think the best time to sit your child on the potty is when he or she is 16-18 months old. However, it's important to be flexible.

BUT DINO
DID NOT UNDERSTAND
WHAT TO DO
WITH THE POTTY.

DINO WAS UPSET
THAT HE HAD
DIRTIED HIS PANTS.

A DINOSAUR MADE
NO FEEL BETTER.
"IF YOU WANT
O POOP OR PEE,"
TOLD HIM SOFTLY,
 SIT ON THE POTTY."

*Tip for parents: Do not scold your child if he makes a mistake.
Just remind him what to do next time.

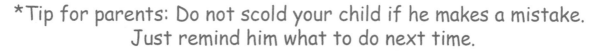

DINO WENT TO PLAY
WITH HIS TOYS.

SUDDENLY HE FOUND
HE WAS SITTING
IN A PUDDLE.
HE HAD JUST PEED
IN HIS PANTS.

DINO WAS UPSET
ABOUT HIS WET PANTS.

DAD DINOSAUR
CALMED HIM DOWN.
"IF YOU WANT TO POOP OR PEE,"
HE REMINDED HIM GENTLY,
"JUST REMEMBER
TO PULL DOWN YOUR
PANTS AND
SIT ON THE POTTY."

DINO WENT TO WATCH TV.
WHILE HE WAS WATCHING
THE CARTOONS, HE
SUDDENLY
WANTED TO POOP.

THE POTTY WAS NEARBY.
SO DINO WENT AND SAT ON IT,
JUST AS MOM AND DAD
DINOSAUR HAD
TOLD HIM.

Tip for parents: Keep the potty close by.

THIS TIME,
DINO WAS VERY HAPPY.
HIS PANTS WERE
CLEAN AND DRY,
AND THE POOP WAS
IN THE POTTY.

Tip for parents: If you have a boy, after he has learned to distinguish between the urge to poop and the urge to pee, teach him to pee standing up.

Please visit us at
ezramonson.com/gift
to download our free coloring pages

Made in the USA
Middletown, DE
27 October 2018